MY FIRST
GERMAN
PHRASES

Good afternoon.
Guten Tag.
(GOOT-en tahk)

Good-bye.
Auf Wiedersehen.
(ouf VEE-der-zayn)

BY
JILL KALZ

ILLUSTRATED BY
DANIELE FABBRI

TRANSLATOR
TRANSLATIONS.COM

PICTURE WINDOW BOOKS
a capstone imprint

TABLE OF
CONTENTS

HOW TO USE THIS DICTIONARY

This book is full of useful phrases in both English and German. The English phrase appears first, followed by the German phrase. Look below each German phrase for help to sound it out. Try reading the phrases aloud.

Topic heading in English

Topic heading in German

Additional phrases to learn

Phrase in English
Phrase in German
(pronunciation)

NOTES ABOUT THE GERMAN LANGUAGE

In German, nouns are written with an uppercase letter. The German word for "the" tells a noun's gender. There are three forms of "the" in German. These are:

  der—used for masculine nouns
  die—used for feminine nouns
    and all plural nouns
  das—used for nouns with
    neutral gender

In German other words also change depending on the noun's gender. Here is a quick reference guide.

English word	Masculine	Feminine	Neutral	Plural
a/an	ein/einen	eine	ein	
my	mein	meine	mein	meine
your	dein	deine	dein	deine

3

LETTERS OF THE ALPHABET
AND THEIR PRONUNCIATIONS

A a • ah	B b • bay	C c • tsay
D d • day	E e • ay	F f • eff
G g • gay	H h • hah	I i • ee
J j • yot	K k • kah	L l • ell
M m • emm	N n • enn	O o • oh
P p • pay	Q q • koo	R r • err
S s • ess	T t • tay	U u • ooh
V v • fow	W w • vay	X x • iks
Y y • IP-si-lon	Z z • tsett	

IT **SOUNDS** *LIKE*

There are 30 letters in the German alphabet. These letters include the 26 letters of the English alphabet. German also uses two dots above the vowels a, o, and u. This umlaut gives these vowels a different sound. In some words, the symbol ß appears. To learn how to say each letter and symbol, look at the chart below.

	SOUND	PRONUNCIATION	EXAMPLES	
CONSONANTS	b	like p in jump when it is the last letter of a word	gelb	gelp
	d	like t in jet when it is the last letter of a word	Mund	moont
	g	sometimes like k in kite	Angst	ahnkst
	j	like y in yes	Jacke	YAK-ke
	s	sometimes like z in zebra if at the beginning of a syllable	Sand	zant
	v	like f in forest	Vogel	FOH-gul
	w	like v in vase	Wasser	VASS-uh
	z	like ts in tsar	Zebra	TSE-brah
	ß	like ss in lasso	Fuß	fooss
VOWELS	a	like ah in ha; before a double consonant then like u in must	Haare / Tasse	HAH-ruh / TUH-ssuh
	e	like e in neck	Decke	DEK-ke
	i	like i in wind	Kind	kint
	o	like o in rocket	Locke	LOK-ke
	u	like oo in food	Blume	BLOO-muh
	ä	like e in men	Länder	LEN-duh
	ö	like ea in learn	schön	shearn
	ü	like ew in news	süß	sews
VOWEL COMBINATIONS	ei	like ye in rye	reiten	RYE-tun
	au	like ou in mouse	Maus	mouse
	äu	like oy in boy	Häuser	HOY-sur
	eu	like oy in boy	heute	HOY-tuh
LETTER COMBINATIONS	sch	like sh in short	schlafen	SHLAH-fuhn
	tz	like ts in Betsy	Katze	CUT-suh
	sp	say as shp	Sport	shport

English: THE BASICS

Hello.
Hallo.
(HAL-loh)

Excuse me.
Entschuldigung.
(ehnt-SHUL-dih-gung)

Good-bye.
Auf Wiedersehen.
(ouf VEE-der-zayn)

Please.
Bitte.
(BIT-tuh)

Good morning.
Guten Morgen.
(GOOT-en MOHR-gen)

Good afternoon.
Guten Tag.
(GOOT-en tahk)

Good night.
Gute Nacht.
(GOOT-uh nahkht)

German: DIE GRUNDLAGEN (dee GROONT-lah-gen)

German: **GEFÜHLE** (geh-FEW-leh)

My <u>stomach</u> hurts.
Mein Bauch tut weh.
(mine bowkh tuht vay)

head
Kopf
(kopf)

leg
Bein
(bine)

arm
Arm
(arm)

I am sorry.
Tut mir leid.
(thut meer lite)

I feel happy.
Ich bin glücklich.
(ikh bin GLOOK-likh)

sad
traurig
(TROW-rik)

angry
böse
(BEH-seh)

MORE TO LEARN

I feel scared.
Ich habe angst.
(ikh HA-buh ahnkst)

9

I live in an apartment.
Ich wohne in einem Apartment.
(ikh VOH-nuh in EYE-nuhm a-PART-ment)

Where do you live?
Wo wohnst Du?
(voh vohnst doo)

a house
ein Haus
(ine hows)

My address is ___.
Meine Adresse ist ___.
(MINE-uh ah-DRESS-uh ist ___)

MORE TO LEARN

My phone number is ___.
Meine Telefonnummer ist ___.
(MINE-uh tel-e-FOHN-num-muh ist ___)

See page 30 for numbers.

English: MEALS

Are you hungry?
Hast Du hunger?
(hasst doo HUN-guh)

I am hungry.
Ich habe hunger.
(ikh HA-buh HUN-guh)

thirsty
durst
(DUHR-st)

What is for supper?
Was gibt es zum Abendessen?
(vas geebt ess tsoom AH-bend-ess-en)

lunch
Mittagessen
(MEE-tag-ess-en)

breakfast
Frühstück
(FROOH-shtook)

MORE TO LEARN

I am not hungry.
Ich habe keinen hunger.
(ikh HA-buh KYE-nuhn HUN-guh)

12

German: MAHLZEITEN (MAHL-tsye-ten)

English: **FAMILY**

This is my mother.
Das ist meine Mutter.
(dahs ist MINE-uh MUHT-er)

This is my aunt and uncle.
Das sind meine Tante und mein Onkel.
(dahs sint MINE-uh TAN-tuh oont mine OHN-kul)

my grandma and grandpa
meine Großmutter und mein Großvater
(MINE-uh GROHS-muht-er oont mine GROHS-faht-er)

Her name is ___.
Sie heißt___.
(zee haist ____)

His name is ___.
Er heißt___.
(err haist____)

German: FAMILIE (fa-MEEL-ih-uh)

Do you speak English?
Sprichst Du Englisch?
(shprikst doo ANG-lish)

Chinese
Chinesisch
(she-NAY-zish)

French
Französisch
(fran-TSOH-sish)

German
Deutsch
(doytch)

Spanish
Spanisch
(SHPAN-nish)

DUTY FREE

7 8 9 10 11

A little.
Ein wenig.
(ine VE-nik)

MORE TO LEARN

father
mein Vater
(mine FAH-ter)

sister
meine Schwester
(MINE-uh SHVES-ter)

brother
mein Bruder
(mine BROO-der)

15

It is time to get up.
Es ist Zeit aufzustehen.
(ess ist tsait OWF-tsoo-shtayn)

What time is it?
Wieviel Uhr ist es?
(VEE-feel oor ist ess)

It is time to go to bed.
Es ist Zeit schlafen zu gehen
(ess ist tsait SHLAH-fun tsoo gayn)

When are we leaving?
Wann gehen wir?
(vahn GAY-en veer)

Happy birthday!
Herzlichen Glückwunsch!
(HERTS-leesh-un GLOOK-voonsh)

When is your birthday?
Wann hast Du Geburtstag?
(vann hahst doo geh-BOORTS-tahk)

My birthday is in May.
Mein Geburtstag ist im Mai.
(mine geh-BOORTS-tahk ist em my)

German: MONATE UND JAHRESZEITEN

(MOH-na-tuh oont YAH-res-tsai-tun)

I love summer!
Ich mag den Sommer!
(ikh mahg dehn ZOM-mehr)

fall
Herbst
(hairpst)

winter
Winter
(VIN-turr)

spring
Frühling
(FROO-ling)

MORE TO LEARN

January
Januar
(YA-noo-ahr)

February
Februar
(FAY-broo-ahr)

March
März
(merts)

April
April
(ah-PRILL)

May
Mai
(my)

June
Juni
(YU-nee)

July
Juli
(YU-lee)

August
August
(ow-GOOST)

September
September
(zepp-TEM-burr)

October
Oktober
(oc-TOH-burr)

November
November
(no-VAM-burr)

December
Dezember
(deh-TSEM-burr)

German: WETTER (VET-turr)

It is cold.
Es ist kalt.
(ess ist cult)

hot
heiß
(haiss)

It is sunny.
Die Sonne scheint.
(dee SOHN-nuh SHY-nt)

Wear a coat.
Trage einen Mantel.
(TRA-ghe EYE-nuhn MAHN-tull)

boots
Stiefel
(SHTEE-fel)

hat
eine Mütze
(EYE-nuh MEET-tsuh)

mittens
Handschuhe
(HANT-shoo)

German: SCHULE (SHOO-luh)

Where is the bathroom?
Wo ist das Badezimmer?
(voh ist dahs BAH-de-tsim-mer)

lunchroom
der Pausenraum
(dare POW-zen-roum)

bus stop
die Bushaltestelle
(dee BOOS-halt-uh-shteh-luh)

Go right.
Gehe rechts.
(gay raks)

left
links
(links)

straight ahead
geradeaus
(gay-ra-duh-OUWS)

Are you ready for the test?
Bist Du bereit für den Test?
(beest doo buh-RITE feer dehn tast)

I forgot.
Ich habe es vergessen.
(ikh HA-buh ess var-GUESS-un)

English: AT HOME

Where are you?
Wo bist Du?
(voh beest doo)

I am in the kitchen.
Ich bin in der Küche.
(ikh bin in dehr KOO-shuh)

bathroom
im Badezimmer
(em BAH-duh-tsim-mer)

bedroom
im Schlafzimmer
(em SHLAF-tsim-mer)

living room
im Wohnzimmer
(em VOHN-tsim-mer)

dining room
im Esszimmer
(em ESS-tsim-mer)

German: ZUHAUSE (TSOO-how-seh)

What did you say?
Was hast Du gesagt?
(vas hahst doo gay-ZAHKT)

Mom is in the garage.
Mama ist in der Garage.
(MA-ma ist in dehr ga-RA-zhe)

Go outside.
Gehe raus.
(gay rouss)

upstairs
die Treppe hoch
(dee TRAP-peh hokh)

downstairs
die Treppe runter
(dee TRAP-peh ROON-turr)

German: **HOBBYS** (HOHB-bees)

What is your favorite book?
Was ist Dein Lieblingsbuch?
(vas ist dine LEEB-lings-bookh)

TV show
Deine Lieblingssendung
(DYE-nuh LEEB-lings-ZEN-dung)

Who is your favorite singer?
Wer ist Deine Lieblingssängerin?
(ver ist DYE-nuh LEEB-lings-ZEN-ger-in)

What is your favorite movie?
Was ist Dein Lieblingsfilm?
(vas ist dine LEEB-lings-FILM)

MORE TO LEARN

Good luck!
Viel Glück!
(feel glook)

Numbers • DIE ZAHLEN (dee TSAH-len)

1 one • **eins**
(ains)

2 two • **zwei**
(tsvai)

3 three • **drei**
(drai)

4 four • **vier**
(feer)

5 five • **fünf**
(feenf)

6 six • **sechs**
(zekhs)

7 seven • **sieben**
(ZEE-ben)

8 eight • **acht**
(ahkht)

9 nine • **neun**
(noyn)

10 ten • **zehn**
(tsayn)

11 eleven • **elf**
(elf)

12 twelve • **zwölf**
(tsvulf)

13 thirteen • **dreizehn**
(DRAI-tsayn)

14 fourteen • **vierzehn**
(FEER-tsayn)

15 fifteen • **fünfzehn**
(FEENF-tsayn)

16 sixteen • **sechzehn**
(ZEKHS-tsayn)

17 seventeen • **siebzehn**
(ZEEB-tsayn)

18 eighteen • **achtzehn**
(AHKHT-tsayn)

19 nineteen • **neunzehn**
(NOYN-tsayn)

20 twenty • **zwanzig**
(TSVAN-tsick)

30 thirty • **dreissig**
(DRAI-tsick)

40 forty • **vierzig**
(FEER-tsick)

50 fifty • **fünfzig**
(FEENF-tsick)

60 sixty • **sechzig**
(ZEKHS-tsick)

70 seventy • **siebzig**
(ZEEB-tsick)

80 eighty • **achtzig**
(AHKHT-tsick)

90 ninety • **neunzig**
(NOYN-tsick)

100 one hundred • **hundert**
(HOON-dehrt)

Colors • **DIE FARBEN** (dee FAHR-ben)

 red • **rot**
(roht)

 orange • **orange**
(or-AHN-shuh)

 yellow • **gelb**
(gelp)

 green • **grün**
(green)

 blue • **blau**
(blouh)

 purple • **lila**
(LEE-lah)

 pink • **rosa**
(ROH-zah)

 brown • **braun**
(brown)

 black • **schwarz**
(shvahrts)

 white • **weiß**
(vais)

READ MORE

FEB 27 2013

Kudela, Katy R. *My First Book of German Words.* Bilingual Picture Dictionaries. Mankato, Minn.: Capstone Press, 2010.

Mahoney, Judy. *Teach Me—Everday German.* Teach Me. Minnetonka, Minn.: Teach Me Tapes, 2008.

Melling, David. *My First Oxford German Words.* New York: Oxford University Press, 2007.

INTERNET SITES

FactHound offers a safe, fun way to find Internet sites related to this book. All of the sites on FactHound have been researched by our staff.

Here's all you do:

Visit *www.facthound.com*

Type in this code: 9781404871540

 **Super-cool stuff!** Check out projects, games and lots more at **www.capstonekids.com**

LOOK FOR ALL THE BOOKS IN THE SPEAK ANOTHER LANGUAGE! SERIES:

MY FIRST FRENCH *PHRASES*

MY FIRST GERMAN *PHRASES*

MY FIRST MANDARIN CHINESE *PHRASES*

MY FIRST SPANISH *PHRASES*

Editor: Katy Kudela
Designer: Alison Thiele
Art Director: Nathan Gassman
Production Specialist: Danielle Ceminsky
The illustrations in this book were created digitally.

Picture Window Books
1710 Roe Crest Drive
North Mankato, Minnesota 56003
www.capstonepub.com

 All books published by Picture Window Books are manufactured with paper containing at least 10 percent post-consumer waste.

Library of Congress Cataloging-in-Publication Data
Kalz, Jill
  My first German phrases / by Jill Kalz ; illustrated by Daniele Fabbri.
    p. cm.—(Speak another language)
  Includes bibliographical references.
  Summary: "Simple text paired with themed illustrations invite the reader to learn to speak German"—Provided by publisher.
  ISBN 978-1-4048-7154-0 (library binding)
  ISBN 978-1-4048-7245-5 (paperback)
  1. German language—Textbooks for foreign speakers—English—Juvenile literature. I. Title.
  PF3129.E5K25 2012
  438.3'421—dc23   2011027197

Printed in the United States of America in North Mankato, Minnesota.
102011   006405CGS12